Wham! Arctic

A Killer Food Chain

by

Sean Callery

Illustrated by Shona Grant

Thank you, Shona Grant for your lovely
drawings.
S.C.

With special thanks to our reader:
Joe Hughes

First published in 2010 in Great Britain by
Barrington Stoke Ltd
18 Walker St, Edinburgh, EH3 7LP

www.barringtonstoke.co.uk

ISBN: 978-1-84299-772-7

Printed in Great Britain by The Charlesworth Group

Intro

The Arctic is the area on the top of the world around the Earth's North Pole.

Most of it is not really land: it is a frozen sea.

Where there is land, it too is frozen and there are no trees so it is very windy.

The ice is not flat: it is blown into hills and mountains.

The Arctic

Everything must eat to stay alive. So every living thing is part of a food chain. This chain is in the Arctic, a huge area of land and sea covered by ice most of the time.

Wham! Goodbye algae, hello krill

Krill are very small sea animals that live in huge swarms.

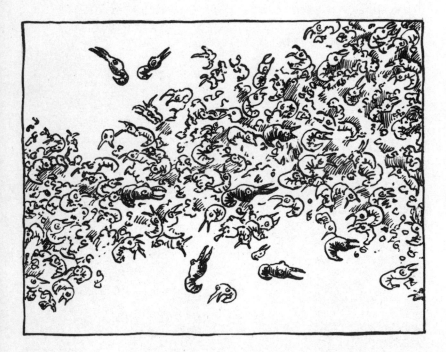

They can swim slowly but most of the time they just float and eat tiny things called algae.

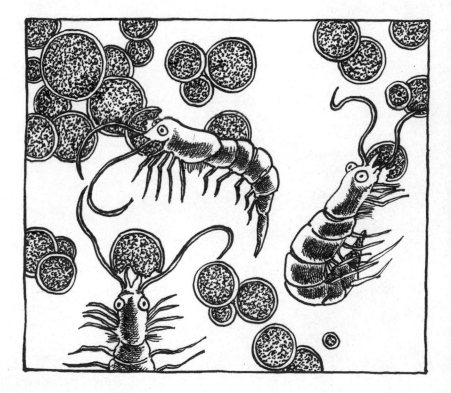

Wham! Goodbye krill, hello polar cod

The polar cod swims far up into the cold north. No other fish goes so far. It can swim as deep as 1000 metres, but most of the time it feeds just under the waves.

Could it kill me?

No, but you would die in the ice-cold seas where it lives. It likes water about as cold as the inside of your fridge.

Wham! Goodbye polar cod, hello ringed seal

Ringed seals dive deep down and can stay under the water for about three minutes. They grab fish with their sharp teeth.

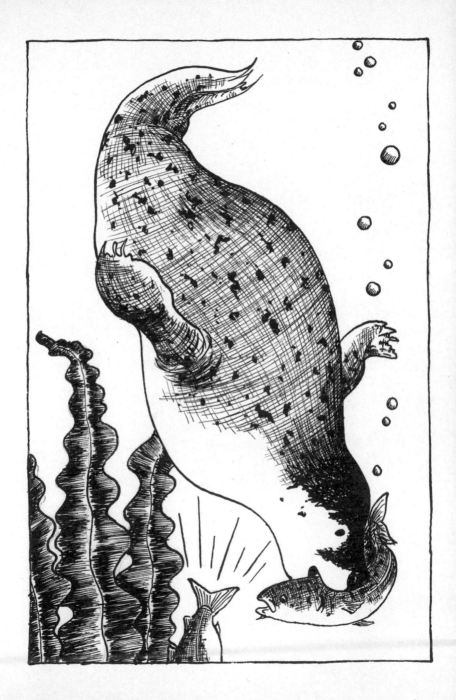

Could it kill me?

No. Humans kill seals and use their skin to make clothes. The meat is fed to dogs.

Wham! Goodbye seal, hello arctic wolf

Wolves are large wild dog-like animals. They hunt in packs and kill by pulling down their prey and biting its neck.

Could they kill me?

Yes, but they don't choose to. Packs of wolves watch and follow polar explorers but they don't often attack them. They are just being nosey.

Wham! Goodbye wolf, hello polar bear

The polar bear is the largest meat-eater on land. It hunts alone and can smell other animals a long way off.

Sniff Sniff

Could it kill me?

Yes. It will creep up on you and if its bite doesn't kill you, then its sharp claws will.

People hunt and eat polar bears but they never eat the liver.

It is poison for humans and for other animals. Even a small amount of polar bear liver will kill a person.

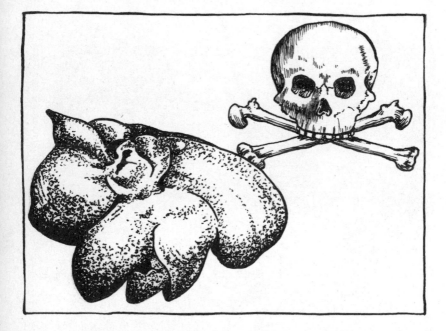

Wham! Goodbye polar bear, hello sea

One day the polar bear will die. Its body will rot and will turn into food for plants on land and in the sea.

Wham! Goodbye Arctic?

People are changing the weather on our planet. This is mostly because we burn fuels such as oil and gas.

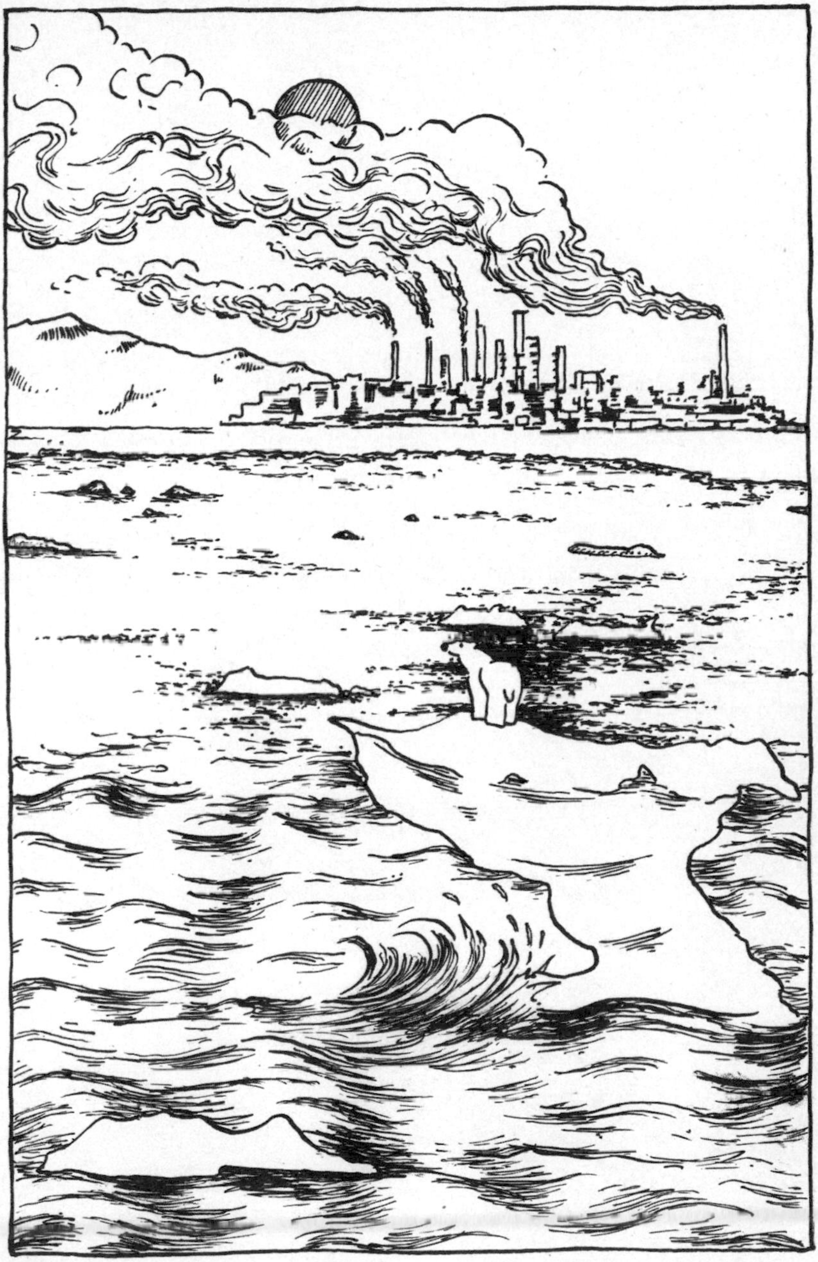

Some Arctic ice freezes in the winter and thaws in the summer. But now more of it is staying melted. This means there is less land for animals like polar bears.

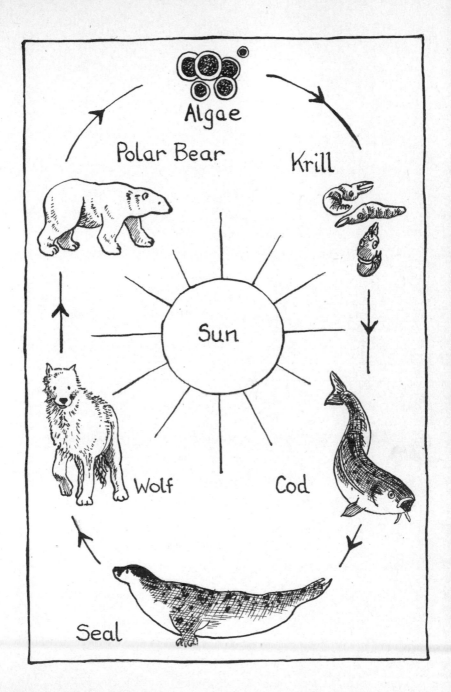

Wham! Fact file

Krill live in such huge swarms that they change the colour of the sea.

The polar cod has special blood that does not freeze.

Seals and polar bears have a thick layer of fat called blubber under their  skin. It keeps them warm.

Wolves howl to talk to each other and to warn others off.

Polar bears are the largest meat-eating animals on land.

WHAM!

Like this book? Why not try the others?

Wham! Rainforest

Killer food chains. Deep in the rainforest.
Life in the rainforest is hard. Everything has to
eat – and everything gets eaten!
From poison dart frogs to jaguars, who comes out
on top?

For more info check out our website:
www.barringtonstoke.co.uk

Watch out for more Wham! books ...

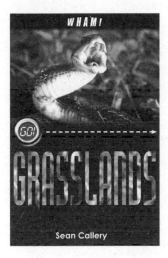

Wham! Grasslands

Life in the plains is hard. Everything has to eat – and everything gets eaten! From grasshoppers to hawks, who comes out on top?

Wham! Undersea

Life under the sea is hard. Everything has to eat – and everything gets eaten! From sea plants to sharks, who comes out on top?

For more info check out our website:
www.barringtonstoke.co.uk